NORFOLK SHIPPING

Norfolk wherries in the 'North River' (Bure), Great Yarmouth about 1880. The medieval tower in the background is a reminder of the port's power in the Middle Ages.

NORFOLK SHIPPING

Michael Stammers

TEMPUS

Acknowledgements

I am grateful to the following people and organisations for the accompanying pictures: Norfolk Museums Service – Great Yarmouth Museum and its curator James Steward,for images on the following pages: p.38 bottom, p.40 all three pictures, p.41, p.55 bottom, p.59 bottom, p.63 bottom, p.107, p.122 top, p.123 top, p.124 bottom, p.125 top and bottom; King's Lynn Museum and its curator Tim Thorpe for p.26 bottom; Cromer Museum for p.21 bottom; the Trustees of National Museums and Galleries on Merseyside Rumbelow Collection for p.13 bottom, p.22 bottom, p.23 top, p.24, p.30 top, p.50 top, p.69 top, p.76, p.82 top and bottom, p.83, p.84 top, p.88 bottom, p.90, p.99 top, p.106 top and bottom, p. 127 top and bottom; Tom Dack p.20 top, p.25 top and bottom; Richard Barham p.43, p.47 top; late Ronald Edwards p.56, p.57 top; David Clement (late Alex Hurst collection) p.52, p.62 top, p.113 top and bottom, p.114 bottom; Andrew Worman p.67 bottom; Adsteam Ltd (formerly Alexandra Towing Co. Ltd) p.115; Malcolm Darch p.126 bottom.

Tempus Publishing Limited
The Mill, Brimscombe Port,
Stroud, Gloucestershire, GL5 2QG
www.tempus-publishing.com

ISBN 0 7524 2757 1

TYPESETTING AND ORIGINATION BY
Tempus Publishing Limited
PRINTED IN GREAT BRITAIN BY
Midway Colour Print, Wiltshire

Contents

After the end of sail, most ships calling at Norfolk ports were owned elsewhere. Here F.T. Everard's *Seniority* is in for repairs and a repaint in 1963.

Introduction

This is a pictorial history about the ships and boats that have been built, owned or sailed to and from Norfolk. It is based on images that come in a wide range of forms: drawings, paintings, prints, photographs, carvings and models. The choice of these images is purely personal and, so far as possible, I have tried to avoid the obvious ones, although in some cases this is difficult. It is also a history of the ships and boats, and not the ports, which have had a good coverage elsewhere. Until the eighteenth century the pictorial record of Norfolk ships is poor. Nevertheless there are images either from the county or from close parallels from other places that can take us back as far as the Middle Ages.

The county of Norfolk is surrounded by water: the North Sea to the east and the north, with the Great Ouse, its tributary the Little Ouse and the Waveney to the west and the south. Then there are the Rivers Yare and Bure, and their tributaries, that flow to the sea at Great Yarmouth. These all became water highways for trade, warfare and, later, leisure. Norfolk has always been an agricultural county with surplus crops to trade and a need to import building materials and fuel. It also lies near to the formerly rich fisheries of the North Sea. The shape of its coast has changed over the centuries. The Yare and Waveney once flowed into a vast estuary with the island of Flegg at its mouth and this gradually silted leaving only Breydon Water. Great Yarmouth developed on a spit of land at its mouth. Some changes have been man-made: the Broads developed from medieval peat diggings and large water areas around the Great Ouse were reclaimed for farming.

Ships and boats played a vital role down the centuries, whether as seagoing traders or humbler inland craft for ferrying or fishing. No doubt the first boats were log boats fashioned from one piece of timber and there is a fragment of one dug up at Smallburgh in the Norfolk Museums Service collection. The Roman naval bases at Brancaster and Burgh show that the Romans were operating warships from Norfolk as protection against Anglo-Saxon sea raiders. Archaeological boat finds and modern replicas give a good idea of the boats of the Anglo-Saxons and the Vikings. Some of their main characteristics, such as clinker (overlapping) planking and pointed, have been inherited by later types of Norfolk boats, especially the wherries and crab boats.

In the Middle Ages Norfolk's sea trade expanded. By 1204, for example, King's Lynn was the fourth highest collector of customs dues in the south-east part of England and it was a port of call for the *cogs* of the German Hanseatic towns. Lynn handled large-scale corn and wool exports drawn not only from Norfolk but also from adjacent counties. Great Yarmouth's fortunes were based around its autumn herring fishery and by the fourteenth century it had become a major export port for worsted cloth – an important Norfolk product in high demand on the Continent. On the north Norfolk coasts smaller ports, such as Blakeney and Cley, and lost ports, such as Wiveton and Snitterley (near Cromer), also flourished, exporting corn and cloth and sending fishing vessels as far north as Iceland. Medieval ships gradually became larger and more complex, with decks instead of being open, doing away with oars and fitting larger masts and sails. By the fifteenth century some Norfolk ships were large *hulcs* with two masts, a bowsprit and high integrated 'castles' at the bow and stern. One of these can be seen carved on the end of a pew in St Nicholas's church, King's Lynn.

By the sixteenth century King's Lynn and Great Yarmouth no longer had the standing of earlier centuries. London dominated overseas exports and the Dutch dominated the North Sea fisheries. Nevertheless both continued to be major ports for the growing coastal trade. The coal trade from the north-east and the delivery of foodstuffs to London were particularly important.

They also had good trading links with the Netherlands and the Baltic. The small 'village ports' also continued to run ships. In 1565, for example, the ports of Blakeney, Cley, Wiveton and Wells owned thirty-four cargo ships and fifteen fishing boats sailing to Iceland. In 1586, a pictorial map of Blakeney harbour was drawn which showed two-masted ships, and a panorama of Great Yarmouth of six years earlier showed not only armed deep-sea merchant ships, but a coastal trader and barges that resemble the later Norfolk wherry.

In the seventeenth century the two great ports thrived in spite of the dislocation caused by the English Civil War and the subsequent wars with the Dutch in the 1660s. Such was their importance that both were included in the Buck Brothers' topographical survey of English towns in the early eighteenth century. Both were shown crowded with ships. Lynn was a significant player in the Greenland whaling trade. The Norwich School of Landscape Artists of the late eighteenth and early nineteenth centuries included ships and boats in many of their compositions. The 'Pier Head' ship painters, who began to flourish from about 1800, painted portraits of particular vessels for their masters or owners who were usually very proud of their ships. Many sailing ships were built in Norfolk and the surviving models and plans give us another type of illustration of local ships.

Norfolk also had its own particular types of fishing boats, and these were first covered in the engravings of E.W. Cooke in his *Fifty Plates of Shipping and Craft* of 1828. His draftsmanship provides an accurate record of these boats before photographs were available.

The first half of the nineteenth century also saw dramatic changes in maritime technology with the development of steam engines, paddles, screw propellers and wrought iron for building ships' hulls. The initial impact was slight; early steamers which used a lot of coal were confined to passenger and 'packet' trades. Steam tugs also became important for getting sailing ships safely in and out of port and for salvage work. Nevertheless many fine sailing ships were built in Norfolk up to the 1870s. Barrels of salted and smoked herrings from Yarmouth to Spain or the Mediterranean (the 'Southern Trade') were an important cargo for such ships as well as the coastal trades. Even the tiny north Norfolk ports of Wells, Cley and Blakeney owned schooners, brigs and barques engaged in the Baltic trades. The spread of steam railways brought competition for bulk commodities such as coal. In 1877, for example, the coal merchants of Cromer stopped importing coal by schooner with the arrival of the Great Eastern Railway. After 1870, there was a slow decline in the number of cargo-carrying sailing ships.

Sailing fishing boats were built in large numbers at Yarmouth, which was a base for trawlers and herring drifters whose numbers were augmented by visiting vessels for the autumn herring fishery. Railways had a positive effect because they could transport fresh fish rapidly to inland towns. The first steam-propelled drifter was launched in 1897 and this led to a boom period and a rapid change to steam. By 1914 there were about 600 steam drifters owned between Yarmouth and its Suffolk neighbour, Lowestoft. The fishery could not sustain such enormous catching capacity and declined rapidly after 1918, and was extinct by the late 1960s.

Steamers took an increasing share of the commercial cargoes from the 1890s onwards. A few steam coasters were locally owned. Sail persisted in the form of the efficient Thames barges which continued to bring cargoes of imported wheat from London until the late 1960s. The Dutch shipbuilders were the first to exploit the economies of marine diesels from the 1920s and their vessels were often seen in Norfolk ports. The same decade saw a growing traffic in petrol to Yarmouth and Lynn. In the 1960s Yarmouth became a base for supply ships for the new North Sea oil and gas industry. However, the coal traffic to the old gas works finished at the same time. Lynn continued to receive a wide range of cargoes delivered to its two docks. Even the port of Wells was kept busy with smaller ships until the 1990s.

Large-scale leisure boating developed in the nineteenth century. At first it was a pursuit for the better-off who could afford their own yachts. Cheap railway fares enabled working-class people to take days out at the seaside or on the Broads, and boat or steamer trips were very popular. The 1880s saw the rise of boat hiring on the Broads. This started with yachts and wherries and boomed after the Second World War with huge numbers of self-drive motor cruisers. Sailing as a sport also grew in popularity. After 1900 cheaper racing dinghies became widely owned and some were of local design and manufacture. The Norfolk Punt, for example, was originally a rigged gun punt (for wild fowling) which, through competitive racing, evolved into one of the most spectacular of all racing boats.

The Norfolk coast, with its treacherous shifting sandbanks and difficult harbour approaches, was dangerous for shipping. Yarmouth Roads was one of the great anchorages in the days of sail and the huge numbers of ships passing through inevitably saw accidents, wrecks and loss of life. This in turn led to marking the main hazards by buoys and lightships, the establishment of lifeboat stations and the rise of the 'beach companies' for salvage work.

The changes since the late nineteenth century have been widely recorded by photographs – another new technology. Images of Norfolk shipping abound after 1880 when the county was seen as a picturesque tourist destination and the images were multiplied by postcards and guidebooks. The late twentieth century saw a growing demand for the preservation of Norfolk's maritime heritage. Fine collections have been accumulated in the Lynn and Yarmouth museums and smaller places, such as Wells and Cromer, have their own maritime collections. Full-size boats including a crab boat, a Lynn 'yoll', an 1820s yacht, wherries, lifeboats and the Lynn-built steam drifter *Lydia Eva* have all been saved. Some Norfolk types such as the beach yawl have become extinct, but the scale models of local model-makers like Phillip Rumbelow of Great Yarmouth provide us with an enduring record of such craft. There is more detail on the various local types of boats in the following chapters.

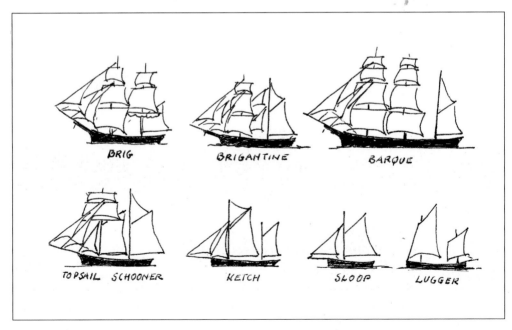

Common rigs of Norfolk sailing ships. See also Chapter 4 – Wherries.

One
Sailing Ships

The Romanized inhabitants of Norfolk in the fifth century feared the raids of the Anglo-Saxon boat peoples, and the *Sae Wylfing* is a modern replica based on the Anglo-Saxon boat burial at Sutton Hoo, Suffolk.

The cargo *knarrs* of the early Middle Ages relied more on sails than oars for propulsion, as these two modern replicas at Roskilde, Denmark, demonstrate. Norfolk's coastal place-names show that there must have been a substantial population using this type of boat.

The next step was the development of larger decked ships – the *cog*. Cogs traded from Germany to Norfolk from the thirteenth century. An intact cog was excavated in the River Weser and conserved by the German National Maritime Museum at Bremerhafen.

The later Middle Ages saw the rise of a different hull design – the *hulc*. This had built-up integral structures at the bow and the stern, often two masts and a bowsprit. There was a splendid carving of one (probably locally owned) on a bench end in St Nicholas church, King's Lynn.

A map of Blakeney harbour in 1586 depicted two and three-masted ships. They were probably built using the new technique, with heavy internal frames and smooth, instead of overlapped, clinker.

A view of Great Yarmouth from the same period showed large armed merchant galleons with gun ports and high superstructures at the stern. It also showed sprit-rigged coasting and river craft which may have been the predecessors of the later Thames barges and Norfolk wherries.

The Buck Brothers' view of Yarmouth in1741 shows a large number of brigs and hoys. The large church is St George's. Note the many vessels out at sea in the Yaremouth Roads.

Hoys were gaff-rigged – i.e. with a main sail rigged along the centre line rather than across as with square sails and with triangular head staysails hoisted on the rigging that supported the mast. They were used extensively for packet services carrying passengers and expensive goods from London to a more or less regular timetable.

The Billy Boy was another type of coaster that originated from the Humber. It retained the older clinker form of construction and was designed for maximum cargo capacity. Quite a few were owned in Lynn, Wells, Blakeney and the very small ports of Brancaster and Burnham Overy.

Right: Later steel ketches built on the Humber retained the name Billy Boy. The *Audrey*, a sailing training ship at Goole, is a replica of one these.

Below: The Billy Boy *Angerona* was one of the last ships to deliver cargoes of coal to Cley in the 1880s.

Left: Thames barges have a diagonal spar (the sprit) to support their main sail. By the nineteenth century they often traded to Norfolk. This one is becalmed on the Yare.

Below: This rig was efficient and only needed a two or three-man crew. This is the *Will Everard* built at Yarmouth in 1925 and sailing into Yarmouth in 1954.

The *Cambria* was still trading under sail alone until 1970. She brought many cargoes to Colman's factory at Norwich.

The *Cambria*, like all Thames barges, had a large windlass to haul the anchors and to help with the lowering of the mast for negotiating fixed bridges.

After the Second World War many barges had their sails reduced and a motor installed. The *Oxygen* at Norwich was typical, with no topmast or mizzen.

Wells Quay, about 1900, shows that commercial sail was still viable, with a local ketch, a three-masted topsail schooner, probably to load barley for Dublin, and a gaff-rigged Thames ('boomie') barge.

18

Another view of Wells of the same era, this time with a whelk boat in the foreground, a local ketch (not the same as in the previous picture), a Billy Boy (possibly the *Blue Jacket* of Blakeney) and a steam coaster.

Schooners were the predominant rig of Norfolk-owned sailing ships in the second half of the nineteenth century. There were five at Lynn about 1880.

Schooners were built in some number in the county. This is the schooner *Minstrel* framed up ready to be planked at Tyrrell's shipyard at Wells in 1847.

The *Minstrel* at Wells, about 1895, showing her deck layout with a tiller instead of a wheel.

The *Minstrel* at Blakeney, about 1905, showed a tubby hull form with a cargo capacity of about 100 tons. Note the Colchester oyster smack in the foreground.

Unloading cargoes on the beach at places such as Cromer, Sheringham and Overstrand was common practice in the summer. The schooner *Ellis* was owned in Cromer.

Some Norfolk schooners were built for foreign trade. The *Norfolk Tar* was a fruit schooner with finer lines and more sails. It carried salted herring from Yarmouth to the Mediterranean and returned with perishable fruit such as grapes and oranges.

Brigs were the most common type of vessel in the early nineteenth century. Yarmouth's busy harbour entrance in 1831 had nothing but brigs and a passing Dutch barge (left).

Brigantines with square sails on the foremast and gaff rig only on the main mast were not so common. Bartlett depicted one on the left of the picture along with a schooner and two wherries with lowered masts.

As competition from railways and steamers grew more intense after about 1870, local sailing ship owners economised by reducing rigs. This saved on maintenance and the number of crew. These brigantines at Yarmouth in 1887 were probably brigs but have lost all their square sails on their main masts.

A brigantine (possibly Scandanavian built) unloading timber into a wherry at Upper Ferry, Southtown, Yarmouth, about 1885.

Above: She was used for deep-sea trade and on one of her calls at a Mediterranean port her owner or master commissioned her from a local artist.

Right: At 151 tons, the *Countess of Leicester* was the biggest ship ever built at Wells when completed in 1847.

Three-masted barques, which were bigger than brigs or schooners, were not so common in Norfolk ports. The *Orkney Lass*, 348 tons, was owned at Wells between 1855 and 1869.

The barque *Arethusa*, 373 tons, was built on the River Nar at Lynn in 1855. Her building and completion was recorded by local artist Henry Baines.

Lynn was an important port for timber coming from the Baltic. This view of Alexandra Dock shows four Scandinavian-built barques that have unloaded timber.

The Finnish barque with the very English name of *Fred* carried timber to Yarmouth in 1923 at a time when sailing ships were rare if not extinct.

Above: The Swedish four-masted schooner *Albatross* brought timber to Yarmouth in the 1950s. Her main role was as a training ship for merchant seamen.

Left: Her rarity attracted many sightseers and she was open for visitors to go on board.

Two
Steamers and Motor Ships

Paddle steamers were the first powered vessels plying Norfolk's waters. This one sailed between Norwich and Yarmouth as a passenger boat in the 1820s.

By the 1840s, paddle steamers such as the *Albatross*, *Cambridge* and *Jupiter* operated regular services from Yarmouth and Lynn to London and Hull.

Screw-propelled steamers became practical in the 1840s but paddle steamers were retained for coastal passenger services and for tugs. Screw steamers became important on coastal routes from the 1870s onwards and this was a London-Dundee steamer calling for cargo at Yarmouth in 1889.

By the late nineteenth century coastal passenger services had been replaced by railways except for the tourist trade. The *Walton Belle* and her sisters ran regular trips from the Thames to Yarmouth from 1890.

The *Southwold Belle* rounds the awkward bend at Gorleston in 1912.

The Belle steamers' regular berth was close to the Town Hall at South Quay with the *Yarmouth Belle* in 1906.

The popularity of the Belle steamers' sea trips was evident in 1912. Note the beautiful brig on the opposite bank.

Nicholsons were Yarmouth tug owners who ran shorter trips. The Edwardian holidaymakers sunning themselves in the 'Cosies' at the Yarmouth harbour entrance watch the *Lord Nelson* and *Lord Roberts* on the outward passage.

One of Nicholsons' steamers (either the *Lord Nelson* or *Lord Roberts*) enters Lowestoft from Yarmouth in 1902, along with a local lug-rigged inshore fishing boat.

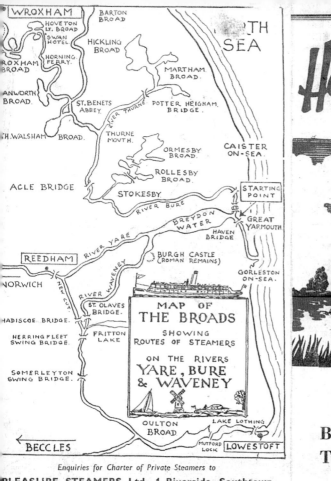

Enquiries for Charter of Private Steamers to

PLEASURE STEAMERS Ltd., 1 Riverside, Southtown

Telephone 2366   **GREAT YARMOUTH**

Member of Great Yarmouth Passenger Shipowner's Association

ALPHAPRINT, QUEEN'S ROAD, GT. YARMOUTH.

River trips were also popular. In the 1950s an all-day trip to Wroxham cost 15s (75p).

The same company also ran harbour trips down to Gorleston in larger vessels with an upper deck and more shelter from South Quay.

The up-river excursions of Pleasure Steamers Ltd of Yarmouth departed from above the bridge at Yarmouth.

All the company's steamers were double-ended for manoeuvrability. Most of the fleet of about six ships like the *Yarmouth* had been built in the 1890s and were still steaming until the early 1960s.

The *Yarmouth Belle*, leaving Norwich, was only forty-eight tons as opposed to the 522 tons of the sea-going paddle steamer of the same name.

Screw-propelled steamers with engines in amidships were increasingly common from the 1860s. This steamer, passing the Sutton swing bridge on the border of Norfolk, was a typical example.

The Ellerman Wilson's line's *Bravo* of 1947 was a late example of this layout, seen here as a rare visitor to Yarmouth, about 1955, and passing the steamer *Norwich Belle* of 1924, inward bound from a trip to see the seals of Scroby Sands.

The smaller cargo steamer (100-200 tons) was rare in Norfolk ports until the early 1900s. They had engines and boiler aft, a single hold and their own cargo handling gear, as seen here at Wells about 1905.

The larger two-hold type with engines aft and bridge amidships was the other main lay-out for cargo coasters. This is a model of the *Sea Nymph*, 246 tons, built for the East Coast Steam Ship Co. of Lynn in 1905.

Diesel engines were first tried on coasters by Dutch shipbuilders in the early 1900s. By the 1930s their efficient motor coasters competed with British steamers. The *David M* was built in 1935 at Groningen, Holland, and in 1960 was owned by Metcalfe Motor Coasters of London.

F.T. Everard was another British coasting firm that made an early change from sail and steam to diesel. Their *Aridity*, built in 1931 at Yarmouth, was a regular coal carrier to Norwich until 1966.

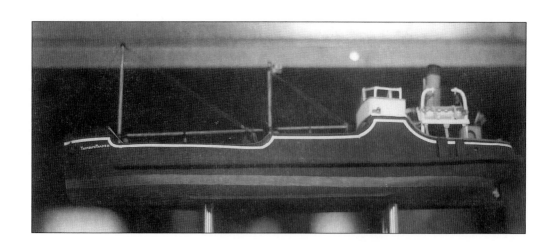

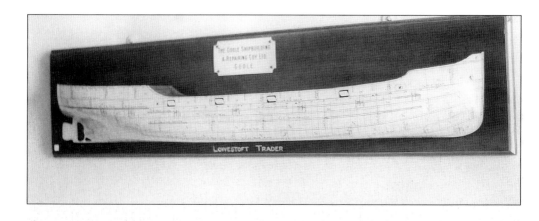

Opposite top: The Yarmouth Shipping Co. was formed in 1906 for a regular cargo service to London. In 1920 they bought the *Yarmouth Trader* second-hand. Her model in the Yarmouth Maritime Museum shows she had two holds with steam engines and bridge both aft – another variation of coaster design.

Opposite middle: In 1934 this company was able to finance a new motor ship, the *Lowestoft Trader*, 380 tons, and the builder's half model for designing the layout of her hull plating is also in the Yarmouth Museum.

Opposite bottom: The *Plover* of 1936 was transferred to Yarmouth from its parent company, the General Steam Navigation Co., in 1960 and was sunk near Rotterdam in 1961.

Another GSN Co. 'bird', the *Grebe*, bound for Yarmouth from the Thames with one man watching. The bridge is typical of a coaster's before the installation of automatic steering.

Foreign coasters bringing timber were seen in large numbers in Yarmouth and Lynn. The *Jell*, 390 tons, was Dutch built in 1955 and seen at Southtown, about 1963.

The Norwegian-flagged timber carrier *Bongo* of 1962 was, at 2,750 tons, one of the biggest ships in Yarmouth in the early 1960s.

The Dutch *Regina*, 313 tons, built in 1951 and sitting on the mud at low tide at Wells about 1970.

Some surviving Thames barges were converted into motor ships. The wooden-hulled *Major* of Whitstable of 1904 delivered a cargo to Colman's at Norwich in 1959.

The *Rogul* was one of the small motor vessels built from the 1960s by the London & Rochester Trading Co. as replacements for their worn-out Thames barges.

The *Success* of 1903 – a steel barge originally called the *Cymric* – had a more drastic rebuild with a full wheelhouse.

Wells received cargoes such as animal feed until 1996. It was put out of business by the increasing size of ships, the silting of the approaches and the small quay space.

Coastal tankers to deliver the products of oil refineries were a new type of coaster after the First World War. Everard's *Prowess*, built in 1926 and weighing 207 tons, delivered oil fuel to the sugar beet factory on the Yare at Cantley.

Oil products have displaced coal as the major coastal traffic. The *Charlotte Theresa* leaving Yarmouth is an 'air draught' design with low superstructure for going under fixed bridges and is registered in Cyprus, a flag of convenience, and not the Red Ensign.

The Dutch coaster *Stern* ashore on Yarmouth is not only a reminder of the hazards of the Norfolk coast but gives a good view of the boxy shape and low profile of modern coasters.

Going aground was a frequent hazard for coasters trading to Norwich, and in some winters, ice was another hazard, as this painting of two trapped Everard coasters shows.

Roll-on roll-off ferry services (ro-ros) for wheeled traffic developed with tank landing ships after the Second World War. Both Lynn and Yarmouth had ro-ro ferry services to the Continent ports which have now been moved to bigger ports. Norfolk Line runs from Folkestone!

Small modern cargo coasters trading to Norfolk, such as Lapthorn's *Anna Meryl* with a cargo capacity of 1,700 tons, are far larger than their predecessors.

Three
Fishing Vessels

The steam drifter is sometimes considered to be the most distinctive Norfolk fishing vessel. By 1914, there were over six hundred registered between Yarmouth and Lowestoft, but the importance of local fisheries goes back to the Middle Ages.

Left: The herring fishery was of great antiquity and, from the late sixteenth century to the mid-eighteenth century, was worked by three-masted square-rigged busses.

Below: The buss was displaced by luggers in the late eighteenth century and E.W. Cooke drew a fine picture of one at South Quay, Yarmouth in 1828.

Most luggers were clinker-built and continued to be built at Yarmouth until the 1870s when they were replaced by carvel-built gaff-rigged dandies. YH 90, the *Sceptre*, was built in 1857 and was replaced by the dandy YH90 *Selina* in 1878.

Luggers, known locally as the 'great boats', were also owned at Cromer and Sheringham, which were both beach ports without harbours.

The dandy YH 857 *Harry* was built at Yarmouth in 1882 and had a combination of a carvel and clinker hull, measured 56ft long and had a tonnage of thirty-four tons. The main mast was lowered at sea when the huge length of drift nets were paid out. A steam-powered capstan invented in 1884 enabled these boats to carry more nets and haul them far more efficiently than doing it by hand.

There were so many boats in the autumn fishery at Yarmouth that they had to berth bow on to the quay, as with YH112 *Orion*, an ex-lugger of 1868.

The Fishwharf Gt Yarmouth.

Steam drifters which docked in the same way were equipped with a derrick to unload the special quarter cran baskets (98lbs/ 44 kilos) quickly.

The autumn catches were immense and eventually unsustainable, but the hundreds of steam drifters became a tourist spectacle advertised by the Great Eastern Railway on its popular series of postcards.

Steam drifters had to be good sea boats. The outward-bound boat at Yarmouth's harbour entrance meets a big wave full on the bow. Note she has her mizzen steadying sail set.

Many drifters were requisitioned by the Royal Navy as minesweepers, as tenders to larger ships and for a whole range of other duties in both world wars.

The herring fishery was in rapid decline in the 1960s. The *Wydale*, built in 1917, was the last wooden steam drifter owned in Yarmouth and went for scrap in 1961.

The visiting Scottish drifters dominated the last years of herring drifting. They were distinctive wooden motor vessels with 'canoe' sterns, all built on the east coast of Scotland.

Above: There were many family-owned boats in ports such as Buckie (BCK) and Wick (WK) where the fishing industry continues, unlike Yarmouth.

Right: The *Lydia Eva* is the only drifter to be preserved. Built at Lynn in 1930 for Easticks of Yarmouth, after only eight years of fishing she became a maintenance tender for a bombing range. In 1970, she was being restored at Yarmouth.

The Jetty at Yarmouth was the historic centre of the fish trade when catches were landed on the beach. The Barking Smack pub at its inland end still stands as a reminder of the busy days when trawlers landed their catches at the Jetty.

Trawlers became an important part of the Yarmouth fishing scene with the arrival of Hewett's 'Short Blue' fleet from Barking on the Thames in the 1850s.

Trawlers drag a bag-shaped net across the seabed and the heavy beam, which kept the mouth of the trawl open, can be clearly seen on this trawler awaiting repairs in 1889.

Trawlers were built and repaired at Southtown and Gorleston on the opposite side of the harbour to Yarmouth. This unusual model of a trawler ready for launching, complete with celebration flags, is part of the collection of the Yarmouth Maritime Museum.

Catches of prime fish, such as cod and plaice, were plentiful in Victorian times. The hardships of a fisherman's life were brought to a wider reading public by R.M. Ballantyne's illustrated novel *The Young Trawler* of 1886.

The Young Trawler was based on the Yarmouth 'Short Blue' trawlers. The most dangerous job was 'boating' the catches to the steamer that took them for auction at Billingsgate Market.

The 'Short Blue' fleet had extensive repair facilities and the *Sequel* was in dry dock in 1889. The wheel steering suggests that she was a fish carrier rather than a trawler. This fleet could not compete with steam trawlers and was laid up in 1901.

Yarmouth had other trawlers besides the 'Short Blues' including smaller cutters such as the *Sultan* of 1877, with a three-man crew and fishing off the Norfolk coast rather than more distant grounds such as the Dogger Bank.

Trawling continued on a limited scale in the twentieth century and even ports like Wells had visits from small trawlers from Essex (for sprats) and Lowestoft. The Scottish-built *May Queen* berthed here in 1973.

In 1890 there was also a fleet of sixty-five distinctive clinker-built shrimpers based at the North Quay on the River Bure. Their main fishing ground was in Yarmouth Roads.

A shrimper under sail in Yarmouth Roads close to an anchored vessel with a trawler to the left.

SHRIMPING AND SMALLBOAT FISHING
An Old Yarmouth Industry

BILLY MOORE   WALTER SPANTON   DARKEY MINNS

The shimpers used a pair of small trawls which they worked sideways using the force of the tide as this drawing from the *Yarmouth Mercury* in 1927 showed.

The shrimpers returning in light winds with all sails set and oars at work in 1889. Note the fine brig drying her sails on the Southtown side of the harbour.

Fresh shrimps were in great demand as a delicacy by Yarmouth's thousands of summer visitors and the traditional type of boat survived under motor well into the twentieth century. The large ship in the background is a Trinity House buoy maintenance tender.

Jack Sheppard was a poor fisherman who used an old smack's boat to dredge for mussels in and among the Yarmouth quays in the 1880s.

Smelt were caught on Breydon water with seine nets set in a circle by a rowing boat and then dragged ashore. The broad-beamed boat is alongside a small houseboat owned by the smelt fishers and the long net has been hung up to dry.

From Caister, north of Yarmouth, there were lug-rigged fishing boats known as punts launched from the beach. They resembled smaller versions of the beach yawls that were maintained there for salvage work. The *Rosebay*, built in 1959, is a motorised version still working from Caister.

To the north of Happisburgh, crab boats were the main type of beach fishing boat. In 1828 (the date of this picture) crabs were caught with netted hoops instead of pots.

The design of these boats, which is probably Viking in origin, has hardly changed in spite of a change from sail to engines and in some cases from wood to fibre glass hulls.

24364 Sheringham Fishermen.

Sheringham, about 1900. The small size of these boats can be seen by the fishermen standing alongside one. Note the crab pots which had an iron base and a netted top. To the right, there are some circular iron traps for catching whelks.

Modern crab boats at Sheringham have been modified with a square stern to take an outboard motor. The two boats in the foreground are *Providence 2* and *My Girls* both built of fibre glass in 1994. The shed on the left houses the historic rowing lifeboat *Henry Ramey Upcher*.

Right: Crab boats could be rowed and carried a large lug sail. One has been preserved at Cromer Museum. This is a model of the *Britannia* built in 1922 and owned by Henry Blogg, the lifeboat hero of Cromer.

Below: At Wells, whelks were caught with pots set from second-hand crab boats. After the Second World War local boat builders produced a 22ft version specifically for the whelkers.

Shell fish such as cockles and mussels were raked from the shore or sandbanks at low tide. Mussel 'canoes' or 'flatties (like the three to the left) were found at Blakeney and Brancaster.

King's Lynn had a fleet of smacks for trawling in the Wash and for seeking whelks along the north Norfolk coast. *48 LN* looks as if she was laid up at West Lynn. There was a topsail schooner at the quay just below the twin towers of St Margaret's church.

There were also smaller 'yolls' for gathering mussels and the *Baden Powell* and the *Kenneth William* have both been preserved by the True's Yard Trust – Lynn's fishing museum.

An extensive inland fishery for eels also existed and at night the long tube of the eel net was stretched across the river.

Freshwater fish as well as eels were caught in Broadland villages, such as Ranworth, from boats with smaller nets known as bow nets.

Four

Wherries

The Norfolk wherry was unique to the eastern rivers of Norfolk and Suffolk. It was normally clinker built. It had a high single sail capable of catching the wind above the trees. Its mast had a large counterweight to enable it to be easily lowered to pass under fixed bridges.

Although there was a wherry-type of vessel in the 1584 view of Yarmouth on page 12, most inland cargoes were carried in square rigged keels. The Buck Brothers' 1741 view of Norwich shows two keels near Bishop's Bridge.

Keels were smaller than wherries and had square sterns. This print from about 1830 shows one laden with tree trunks at Thorpe with a wherry in the background.

Opposite top: The heavily-loaded wherry *Primus*, alongside some baulks of timber at Cobholm, is ready for inland voyage possibly down the Waveney to Bungay, to Norwich along the Yare or to the northerly towns of Aylsham and North Walsham via the Bure or the Ant.

The tide is right and the wherries have worked down the harbour and under the Haven Bridge using punt poles known as quants. Two wherries have raised their masts and set sail.

The wherry's huge tanned sail could be raised by one man using the winch at the foot of the mast.

Having set sail from Yarmouth, a wherry had to cross the shallow waters of Breydon Water.

A wherry running before the wind off Reedham, an important village on the Yare where many wherries were built by the Hall family.

Wherries were built in small yards with a few hand tools and a great deal of skill. This new wherry was being fitted out at Stalham.

Wherries could sail close to the wind. This wherry is off Whitlingham with the wind on the beam. A day sailing yacht has been laid up for winter on the left bank.

Thorpe Reach, Norwich — Valentines Series

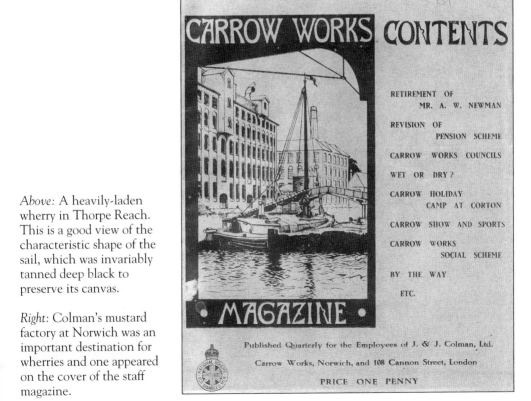

Vol. XVII. No. 1.   OCTOBER, 1923.

CARROW WORKS CONTENTS

RETIREMENT OF
MR. A. W. NEWMAN

REVISION OF
PENSION SCHEME

CARROW WORKS COUNCILS

WET OR DRY?

CARROW HOLIDAY
CAMP AT CORTON

CARROW SHOW AND SPORTS

CARROW WORKS
SOCIAL SCHEME

BY THE WAY

ETC.

MAGAZINE

Published Quarterly for the Employees of J. & J. Colman, Ltd.

Carrow Works, Norwich, and 108 Cannon Street, London

PRICE ONE PENNY

Above: A heavily-laden wherry in Thorpe Reach. This is a good view of the characteristic shape of the sail, which was invariably tanned deep black to preserve its canvas.

Right: Colman's mustard factory at Norwich was an important destination for wherries and one appeared on the cover of the staff magazine.

A wherry off Thorpe village with a cargo of timber that was carried stacked well above the hatches.

A wherry loaded with timber has just passed under Foundry Bridge, Norwich. The wherryman is using a quant to propel her while the mast is down.

Acle Bridge with a mail coach passing and a small wherry with gaff lowered coming in to tie up. The discs in the upper part of the sail are puzzling.

Acle in the 1890s was still a popular calling place for wherrymen before tackling the last winding stretch of the River Bure down to Yarmouth.

The *Meteor* at the Bridge Inn, Acle, weighed twenty-seven tons and was built at Surlingham.

The cement works at Burgh on the Waveney was another source of cargo for wherries.

The *Cornucopia* at Bramerton was a small twenty-ton wherry built at Stalham in 1893.

Wherrymen at Southtown about 1880. Note the unusual square stern wherry in the foreground. The large building on the left advertises 'John Lee Barber & Son's Talisman motor and engine oils'.

A wherry tied up for the night and the smoke from the cabin stove indicates that supper is underway.

A close-up of the same wherry taken sometime later, with the skipper smoking a leisurely pipe – an idyllic scene that appealed to a Victorian photographer.

Wherries and their crews may have seemed picturesque to summer visitors but life in the winter was harsh and when ice blocked the river there would be no wages.

Two wherries attempted to pass on the Ant. One skipper has lowered his gaff to slow his boat while the crew are pushing their craft sideways with quants to make room for the oncoming and heavily-loaded vessel.

A wherry unloading at Stalham, the sail has been swung out of the way and the curved hatch covers have been piled up at each end of the hold. Most wherries carried planks, barrows and shovels for handling the cargoes.

Two wherries at Barton Staithe; the patched sail is a reminder that wherry owners, especially skipper-owners, had to be frugal in order to wring a living from carrying low-paying freights.

Coltishall, the village just before the first set of locks taking the Bure Navigation up to Aylsham, was the location of Allen's Yard which built the last trading wherry, the *Ella*, in 1912.

Geldeston lock was the first of three locks on the River Waveney through which wherries passed to reach the Suffolk town of Bungay. Masts had to be lowered in the lock. Note the fine rowing skiffs (probably for hire) in the foreground.

The same scene in the winter. Note the flooded water meadows. The wherry is raising the sail after passing through the lock.

Wherries rapidly decreased in numbers after the First World War. A few were given motors and the forty-ton *Lord Roberts* was still carrying cargoes (mainly sugar beet) in the early 1960s.

The *Lord Roberts* at Potter Heigham about 1960. The mast was retained for lifting purposes and not for carrying a sail.

The wherry's decoration was distinctive and colourful, and included a decorative wind vane and name boards. The *Zulu* was a twenty-ton wherry owned at Catfield by a Mr Riches.

Two trading wherries have been preserved and still sail, and there are some excellent scale models. The *Gleaner*, being admired by Liverpool schoolboys in 1940, was built by the late Phillip Rumbelow of Yarmouth. This fine model was lost in the 1941 blitz and replaced by Phillip who made an even finer model in the 1970s.

Five

Yachts and
Pleasure Boats

Pleasure boating started as a pursuit of the wealthy. This is a stretch of the River Yare at Norwich with an aristocratic row barge and three other leisure rowing boats in 1741.

W.H. Smith's yacht *Madge* crossing the finish line at Coldham Hall regatta in about 1900. Note the huge amount of sail these single-masted cutters carried.

The *Greyhound* was probably the best of the later nineteenth-century yachts. She won 175 first prizes between 1889 and 1894. Her slender hull was 34ft long but only 6ft wide, with four tons of lead on her keel.

Opposite top: 'Water frolics' or regattas, with sailing and rowing races and much drinking and betting on the results, were popular holiday events in the early nineteenth century. Note the mixture of yachts, rowing boats and wherries, including one of the famous lateen yachts on the left.

Opposite below: Coldham Hall regatta on the River Yare about 1890 with only a slight breeze and a trading wherry threading its way through the racing boats.

Match racing between two yachts was popular as this race at Horning about 1886 between an older lugger and a cutter demonstrates. Yachts of this size would often have paid crews.

Many more people enjoyed the waterways in rowing boats. At Horning in about 1907 a gun punt, a skiff and a miniature wherry pull away from the bank.

William Thompson, boat builder of King Street, Norwich, had rowing boats to let, such as the elegant skiff outside his boat shed. The boat, worked by a single scull over the stern, appears to be more of a ferry for the Steam Packet Inn, whose name is a reminder of an earlier time when the fastest way to Yarmouth was by steamer.

The River Wensum above the head of the navigation at New Mills was known as the 'back river' and was safe for rowing ladies away from the dangers of wherries and coasters.

Yachting became more widespread as small open racing dinghies of standard size grew in popularity around 1900. Declining commercial ports such as Blakeney took on a new role as centres of sailing.

Lug-rigged dinghies racing at Wells, about 1920.

Angling was encouraged by Victorian guidebooks to the Broads. A boat was often needed because of the marshy banks. This gentleman, complete with solar topee, is hoping for a bite at Horsey Mere in a refined version of a reed lighter.

Possibly from a lower social class, but ridiculously over-dressed by today's standards, this bowler-hatted duo have staked their skiff on a bend in the River Bure. It was probably too calm for a big catch.

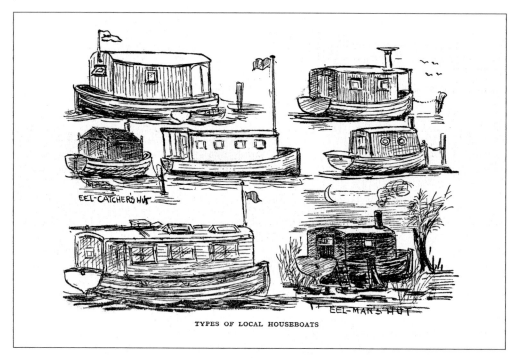

TYPES OF LOCAL HOUSEBOATS

Some visitors wanted to stay on the Broads and took to houseboats. Those with little money might buy an old ship's boat and build a shed over it. Arthur Patterson, the famous author, and illustrator of the wildlife of Norfolk, drew this delightful sketch in 1928.

This was a former beach yawl that was used by the painter T.F. Goodall and the photographer P.H. Emerson in the late 1880s.

The twenty-seven ton North Walsham wherry *Elizabeth* ended up as a houseboat at Thorpe.

The shortage of housing after the Second World War saw the conversion of a variety of boats into floating homes. This former motor gunboat was a well-kept and striking feature of the river at Thorpe for many years.

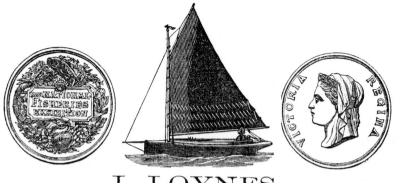

J. LOYNES,

BOAT BUILDER, Elm Hill, NORWICH,

HAS AT HIS

Boating Station, Wroxham Bridge,

YACHTS AND BOATS FOR HIRE,

John Loynes was one of the pioneers of the boat hire business on the Broads and, shortly after this 1888 advert, moved his whole establishment from Norwich to Wroxham and expanded the business from building open boats to cruising yachts.

Ernest Collins was another pioneer of hiring cruisers. This advertisement shows his fleet at his Wroxham yard about 1900.

Motor boats began to make an impact in the hire business in the 1920s. By the 1950s they formed the majority of the hire fleets.

Accommodation on local yachts ranged from luxurious panelled and carpeted cabins to a simple canvas awning flung over the spars as in the case of this yacht at Potter Heigham.

The end of a cruise at Yarmouth. The 'crew' were all smartly dressed, perhaps ready to board the train at the nearby Southtown station back to London.

A cruising yacht towing its tender on Wroxham Broad about 1890. Note the tall topmast. Hired yachts of this type usually came with a paid crew, with the skipper probably acting as cook and steward as well.

On The Bure Wroxham

Trading wherries were sometimes converted into hire yachts for the summer. They were recommended if there were ladies in the boating party.

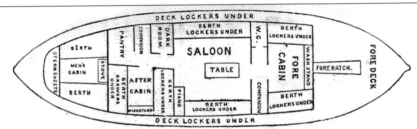

They offered much more space than any yacht, with a fore cabin, which could be used by the women, and a piano for evening entertainment in the saloon.

104

D. 30659. WHERRY LEAVING WROXHAM.

Some trading wherries were permanently converted into pleasure craft and could be distinguished by the built-up hatches with windows and white sails.

The *Bertha* was a twenty-ton wherry trading to North Walsham before conversion to a yacht in the late 1890s. She made a fine sight sailing close-hauled.

The *Britannia* at Belaugh. The black sail suggests that she was converted back to trading in the winter. There were four wherries called *Britannia* and it is not clear which one this was.

The *Bramble* was built as a pleasure wherry. There were also wherry-rigged yachts.

The pleasure wherry *Ecila* (*Alice* spelled backwards) at Yarmouth dressed overall possibly for a regatta.

The *Jenny Lind* was a unique variation of the pleasure wherry, a steam-powered day trip vessel built in 1879 by Halls of Reedham to run excursions between Norwich and Bramerton Woods.

Thorpe features rather a lot in this selection but this view shows the typical wooden motor boats built here and other hire centres such Wroxham and Potter Heigham. The pleasure wherry *Dragon* can be seen in the background.

For those who could only afford day trips to the seaside there were exciting sailing trips from the beach at Gorleston and Yarmouth in specially designed pleasure boats.

The Beach, Newport, Near Hemsby.

FRITH
HMY 78

JUNO   MORSTON

Above: The resort villages that developed to the north of Yarmouth saw local fishermen using the boats for sea trips in the summer months.

Right: The *Juno* is another north Norfolk day sailing venture. She is a ketch-rigged barge built of steel on the lines of a Thames barge.

The *Albatross* is a Dutch clipper built in 1899 which delivered the last commercial cargo to Wells and is based in the port now to provide sea trips and sail training.

Six

Tugs and
Service Vessels

The first tugs were paddle steamers and appeared in Norfolk ports in the 1840s. The *Flying Childers* was similar to the *Economy* of Wells, which was bought from her builders at North Shields in 1840.

Yarmouth had a large tug fleet to cope with the increasing number of fishing vessels.

The *Tom Perry* towing six Scottish 'zulus' to sea. One thrifty skipper has made his crew row their lugger out of the harbour. The *Tom Perry* had been built at South Shields in 1879 and came to Yarmouth in 1888.

The *Reaper* in charge of three Yarmouth drifters who have set most of their sails before arriving at the harbour entrance.

Another paddle tug, possibly the *United Service*, tows a brigantine in ballast and two fishing smacks to sea.

The *Richard Lee Barber* was the last steam tug at Yarmouth. Built at Fellows Yard in 1939, it was scrapped in 1964. In 1963 she towed the large Greek steamer *Pothoula II*.

The *United Service* was the most well-known Yarmouth tug. Built at North Shields in 1871 and not broken up until 1942 this tug was often used for salvage work and rescued the Danish *Annie* in 1888.

The diesel tug *Brightwell*, built in 1981, was among the last ships ever built at Yarmouth. It was designed to handle the large container ships using the port of Felixstowe.

The *Cypress* and the *Gensteam* were two smaller steam tugs operated by the Great Yarmouth Shipping Co. mainly for towing barges. Here the *Cypress* is passing the Dutch coaster *Confiance* at Read's Mill, Norwich.

In the foreground are some of the forty-five ton steel barges towed by the *Cypress* and the *Gensteam*. The *Richard Lee Barber* has a tricky job to ease the bow of the *Pothoula II* clear of the *Seniority*.

Ferries were found instead of bridges in many Norfolk villages. Pull's Ferry at Norwich was probably amongst the oldest. It was propelled by hauling on a chain laid across the river.

The reed lighter was the other work boat of the Broads. This was of broad, shallow draft and clinker-built and could carry a huge stack of cut Norfolk reeds which were a noted roofing material.

The ferry at Martham in 1913 on the River Thurne was more of a floating bridge that could carry vehicles.

The Fen lighters on the Great Ouse were of a different design to the wherry. They were up to 47ft long and carried about twenty tons and were usually towed in gangs of three or more. These lighters were tied up at Thetford, about 1900.

More of the barges owned by the Great Yarmouth Shipping Co. in the foreground. Most had been built at Gainsborough in the early 1900s to replace wherries. The tanker *Apricity* passing through Haven Bridge is a reminder of the growing importance of the offshore oil and gas industry to Norfolk shipping.

The North Sea oil industry grew rapidly from the mid-1960s and Yarmouth was the home port for many specialised service ships. The *Vestfonn*, 3,753 tons, was built as an oil rig supply ship in 1983 and later converted into an oil well stimulation vessel.

The muddy rivers draining into the sea at Yarmouth and Lynn carried tons of silt into the harbours which had to be dredged to allow ships free passage and safe berths. The steam bucket dredger *Fitzroy* was deployed at Yarmouth.

Another view of the *Fitzroy* showing the folding chutes to port and starboard for dumping the dredgings into barges or, in this case, wherries. These would be towed out to sea for dumping.

Opposite below: King's Lynn has its own body of Conservators who are responsible for buoying the Ouse channel and who run the modern buoy tender *Saint Edmund*, which is fitted with hydraulic lifting equipment instead of derricks.

There were numerous dangerous shoals and sandbanks off the Norfolk coast which were surveyed and marked with buoys by Trinity House. They had a maintenance depot at Yarmouth graced by the figurehead from their steam tender *Irene* of 1890.

Trinity House also maintained lightships to mark the most important hazards. This is a delightful nineteenth-century model of the St Nicholas lightship stationed off Yarmouth. The oil-lit lantern was hoisted up the tall mast.

Lightships have been replaced by automatic buoys, but their heavy build makes them ideal for other uses and here a lightship replaced an ex-motor torpedo boat as the Sea Scout headquarters.

Many sailing ships were lost and many sailors drowned, especially in the winter gales. In 1888 the *Vauban*, a French barque, came ashore at Yarmouth. A chain of lifeboat stations was established from Huntstanton to Gorleston.

The Norfolk and Suffolk type of sailing lifeboat was designed for launching from beaches and was self-righting. This lifeboat is being hauled out to sea by its crew.

Lifeboat Day, probably at Yarmouth, in 1906. The Royal National Lifeboat Institution relied on donations from its establishment and Lifeboat Days were popular events. In addition to the lifeboat stationed on the beach, there was a station in the harbour and a private lifeboat owned by a company of beachmen.

The Hunstanton lifeboat *Licensed Victualler* was launched by horses from local farms. In 1920 this station took part in trials of one of the first crawler tractors.

Many Norfolk lifeboatmen performed heroic rescues and nowhere more so than at Caister. In 1973 when the RNLI decided that Caister would only have an inshore boat, funds were raised to buy the *Shirley Jean Adye* which was then replaced by the *Bernard Matthews* in 1991.

The fierceness of the gales is captured in this picture of the Gorleston lifeboat returning from rescuing the crew of the steamer *Fox* on 27 November 1924.

Companies of beachmen from Yarmouth beach north to Happisburgh sailed large lug-rigged beach yawls to service the huge number of sailing ships passing through Yarmouth Roads in the nineteenth century. Note the lookout tower.

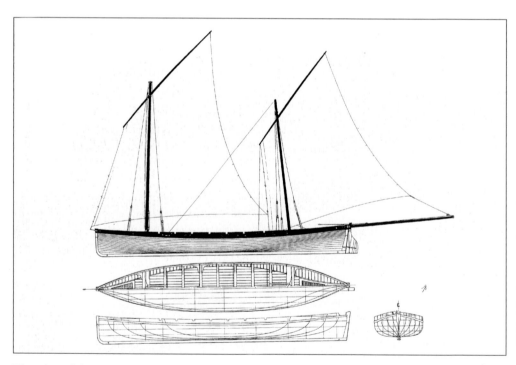

The plan of the *Georgiana* of 1892 shows the fine lines of the clinker-built hull and the huge sail area. Yawls carried as many as forty crew members, if attending a salvage job, who could also row and act as ballast.

No yawl has survived and only the rudder of the *Bittern* is preserved at Southwold. There are some fine models including one by the late Phillip Rumbelow depicting the Winterton yawl *Band of Hope*.

Besides the yawls the beachmen had smaller gigs for short runs and excursion boats for holidaymakers. I suspect this picture may have been taken at Lowestoft but it shows the graceful hull shape.

The mission ship *Sir William Archibald* sailed with the local fishing fleet to attend to the fishermen's spiritual and social welfare. There was a particular problem with Dutch 'copers' selling large quantities of spirits to fishermen at sea.

Even the old and abandoned ship can perform a useful service. This ancient schooner has been sunk in Breydon Water to help maintain the main channel.